Graveyard Laughter

GRAVEYARD LAUGHTER

compiled by

Samuel Klinger

SATELLITE BOOKS: London

First published in Great Britain 1979
by Satellite Books (Publishers), Kendall
House, 9 Kendall Road, Isleworth, Middlesex.

ISBN 0905186974

Made and printed in Great Britain by
The Garden City Press Limited
London and Letchworth.

In Memory of My Mother

FOREWORD

Britain has always been a fascinating country for foreigners, even for those who have lived only a stone's throw away from this island. Continentals have found here customs and traditions which were greatly different from those of their native lands.

When I came to Britain before the last war, I was immediately enchanted by many of her strange traditions, and to this day this country has retained for me the charm of a magic island.

Some years ago when I accidentally came across a book of humorous British epitaphs, its contents, at first, appeared to me a work of pure fiction. But when I later saw a short documentary film showing tombstones with humorous inscriptions, I realised with astonishment that nothing was impossible in this country.

It is well known abroad that the British like to laugh about themselves, but their humour goes even beyond the grave, something which has never been noticed in any other nation.

Some races, especially the Jews, have long ago learned to laugh about themselves. Sigmund Freud in his book *Jokes and their Relation to the Unconscious* even went so far as to state that he did not know any other people who could make fun of their own to such a degree as the Jews. But Jewish humour stops at the grave. None of their tombstones has ever borne a humorous inscription. Jewish cemeteries are solemn places. So it is with many other nations. None of them would ever tolerate levity on their graveyards. We may find witty epitaphs in countries outside Britain, especially the U.S.A., but these have been introduced by British immigrants or have an Anglo-Saxon flavour.

Humorous epitaphs in Britain date back to many centuries. We find them as early as the fourteenth century, they appear frequently in later periods and seemed to have reached their peak in the eighteenth century. During the nineteenth century they become less frequent, and have disappeared completely in the twentieth due to intervention by the Law and the Church. This action was probably justified because some inscriptions made unflattering remarks about the dead who were not able to reply. Some were even offensive or obscene.

It may perhaps surprise the reader to learn that the eighteenth century, which was certainly not a happy period in British social history, had an abundance of amusing epitaphs. But humour has never been dormant, not even in times of adversity.

These epitaphs represent a great variety of types of humour. Some are punning, others have a double meaning; many are cynical or derogatory, a few are even obscene. It may be interesting to note that some authors of the Victorian era who wrote comprehensive books on graveyard humour often omitted from their works blasphemous and obscene epitaphs. These appeared more frequently in books of the

8

eighteenth century and the later years of the twentieth century.

It is not surprising that women have been the main target of such epitaphs. Since ancient times women have been the butt of jokes and unjustified derision, and they still are. To make fun of their wives or mothers-in-law is part of the regular stock-in-trade of most of today's comedians. I have therefore devoted the first chapter of this book to epitaphs on women and have then continued to arrange the inscriptions according to the counties under their old original names and boundaries.

Often mentioned in other books are amusing tombstone inscriptions whose authenticity is open to question because the graveyards in which they are supposed to be located are not named. Nevertheless it is possible that some of these epitaphs could be genuine. On the whole the 'doubtful' epitaphs are to be found in the chapter "Truth and Fiction" but others of the same nature relating particularly to women, have been included in the chapter "Ladies First".

These epitaphs have been gathered from literature across three centuries. The earlier books used the old English spelling, authors of later periods used the modern spelling. I quote the inscriptions as I found them, and I hope the reader will not feel confused when he finds epitaphs of any particular period in both old and modern spelling.

Epitaphs have attracted many writers and historians, past and present. At the beginning of this century the British Museum contained over two hundred books on this subject, and we may safely assume that these have been added to since then. It is only regrettable that so little thought has been given to the preservation of tombstones bearing humorous inscriptions although they present unique examples of the British heritage. Exposed to the elements throughout centuries, a great number of these stones suffered such erosion that their inscriptions became illegible. Other tombstones, equally valuable, have disappeared completely from many graveyards. It is beyond my competence to make any recommendations regarding the preservation of such monuments. Perhaps the present high standard of photography could prove the means of preserving some of the still legible inscriptions before time and weather effect their total obliteration.

Humberside, 1979   SAMUEL KLINGER

Friend in your epitaph I'm grieved,
So very much is said:
One half will never be believed,
The other never read.
An Old Epitaph.

LADIES FIRST

Ribbesford, Bewdley, Worcester

On the wife of the Parish Clerk

The children of Israel wanted bread,
And the Lord he sent them manna.
Old clerk Wallace wanted a wife,
And the devil sent him Anna.

Beneath this stone lies Katherine my wife,
In death my comfort, and my plague through life,
Oh! Liberty – but soft, I must not boast;
She'll haunt me else, by jingo, with her ghost.

St. Albans, Hertfordshire

Mary Gwynne

Here lies the body of Mary Gwynne,
Who was so very pure within.
She cracked the shell of earthly sin,
And hatched herself a cherubim.

East Hornden, Essex

Martha Tyrell, 1690

Could this stone speak, it would the reader tell
She that lies here did her whole sex excell:
And why should death with a promiscuous hand
In one rude stroke impoverish a land.

Bury St. Edmunds, Suffolk

Jane Kitchen

Here lies Jane Kitchen
Who when her glass was spent,
She kicked up her heels,
And away she went.

Churchyard near Canterbury, Kent

Of children in all she bore twenty-four;
Thank the Lord there will be no more.

Haddington, Scotland

If Chastity commends a Wife,
And Providence a Mother,
Grave Modesty a Widdow's Life,
You'll na find sick another
In Haddington, as Marion Gray!
Who here does lye till Domis-day.

Here rest my Spouse; no pair through life
So equal liv'd as we did;
Alike we shar'd perpetual strife,
Nor knew I rest till she did.

Old Gray Friers, Edinburgh, Scotland

Here snug in Grave my wife doth lie
Now she's at Rest, and so am I.

Northampton

Here lies the corpse of Susan Lee
Who died of heartfelt pain;
Because she loved a faithless he,
Who loved not her again.

Chester, Cheshire

On a woman who kept a potter's shop in Chester

Beneath this stone lies the old Katherine Gray
Chang'd from a busy Life to lifeless Clay.
By Earth and Clay she got her Pelf,
Yet now she's turned to Earth herself.
Ye weeping friends, let me advise,
Abate your Grief, and dry your Eyes,
For what avails a Flood of Tears?
Who knows, but in a Run of Years,
In some tall Pitcher, or broad Pan,
She in her Shop may be again?

Warrington, Lancashire

Margaret Robinson, 1816

This maid no elegance of form possessed;
No earthly love defil'd her sacred breast;
Hence free she liv'd from the deceiver man;
Heaven meant it as a blessing; she was plain.

Fifeshire churchyard

Here lies my gude and gracious Auntie
Whom Death has packed in his portmanty.

Kent

Sixteen years a Maiden
One twelve Months a Wife,
One half hour a Mother
And then I lost my Life.

Staverton, Gloucestershire

Here lies the body of Betty Cowden
Who would live longer but she couden;
Sorrow and grief made her decay,
Till her bad leg carried her away.

Grantham, Lincolnshire

> Here lies returned to clay
> Miss Arabella Young
> Who on the first of May
> Began to hold her tongue.

Stanwell, Middlesex

> Nere to this spot my wife is layd,
> At rest from all her earthly laburs.
> Glorrie to God, peece to the ded
> And to the years (i.e. ears) of all her nayburs.

Wilton, Wiltshire

Elizabeth Bell, 1725

> At twenty years of age I little thought,
> That hither to this place I should be brought,
> Therefore as in the Lord I put my Trust,
> I hope I shall be blest among the Just.

Anna Lovett

> Beneath this stone & not above it,
> Lie the remains of Anna Lovett,
> Be pleased good reader not to shove it,
> Lest she should come again above it.
> For 'twixt you & I, no one does covet
> To see again the Anna Lovett.

Saratoga, U.S.A.

Mary Ricular, 1792

Here lies the wife of Robert Ricular
Who walked the way of God Perpendicular.

St. Pancras, London

On a Maid of Honour

Here lies (the Lord have mercy on her!)
One of her majesty's maids of honour:
She was young, slender and pretty;
She died a maid – the more the pity.

King Stanley Churchyard, Gloucestershire

Ann Collins, 1804

'Twas as she tript from cask to cask,
In at a buny-hole quickly fell,
Suffocation was her task,
She had not time to say farewell.

St. Leonard's Foster Lane, London

On an Old Maid, 1750

Beneath this silent stone is laid
A noisy antiquated maid,
Who from her cradle talked till death,
And ne'er before was out breath.

Dalkeith, Scotland

Margaret Scott, age 125 years, 1738

Stop passenger, until my life you read;
The living may get knowledge by the dead.
Five times five years I liv'd a virgin's life;
Ten times five years I was a virtuous wife;
Ten times five years I liv'd a widow chaste;
Now weary of this mortal life, I rest.
Between my cradle & my grave had been
Eight mighty Kings of Scotland & a Queen;
Four times five years the Common-wealth I saw,
Ten times the subjects rose against the law.
Twice did I see old Prelacy pull'd down,
And twice the cloak was humbled by the gown.
An end of Stewart's race I saw; nay, more!
My native country sold for English ore:
Such desolations in my life have been,
I have an end of all perfection seen.

Here lies my wife,
Here lies she
Hallelujah
Hallelujee.

Norwich, Norfolk

On a Domestic Servant

Here lies a poor woman who was always tired,
She lived in a house where help wasn't hired:
Her last words on earth were: "Dear friends, I am going
To where there's no cooking, or washing, or sewing,
For everything there is exact to my wishes,
For where they don't eat there's no washing of dishes.
I'll be where loud anthems will always be ringing,
But having no voice I'll be quit of the singing.
Don't mourn for me now, don't mourn for me never,
I am going to do nothing for ever and ever."

Hadleigh, Suffolk

Susan Pattison, 1706

To free me from domestic strife
Death called at my house, but he spoke with my wife.
Susan, wife of David Pattison lies here,
Stop Reader, and if not in a hurry, shed a tear.

Norwich, Norfolk

1679

Sarah York this life did resigne
On May the 13th, 79

Ilfracombe, Devon

Joan Ley, 1759

Joan Ley here she lays all mould in grave
I trust in God her soul to save.
And with her Saviour Christ to dwell
And there I hope to live as well.

Orpington, Kent

Mary Smith, 1755

Here lies Mary, never was contrary
To me nor her neighbours around her.
Like Turtle and Dove we lived in love
And I left her where I may Find her.

Written by Jaques Loxen on his scolding wife.

Here lies my wife, and Heaven knows
Not less for mine than her repose.

Written by the poet Dryden to the memory of his wife.

Here lies my wife, here let her lie;
Now she's at rest, & so am I.

From a Yorkshire Churchyard

Here lies my poor wife without bed or blanket
But dead as a doornail, God be thanked.

Jersey

On a Fat Woman

"All flesh is grass"
The Scriptures they do say,
And grass when dead
Is turned into hay.
Now when the reapers her away do take,
Moi what a wopping haystack she will make.

Gloucestershire

Here lies poor Charlotte
Who died no harlot;
But in her virginity,
Of the age nineteen,
In this vicinity,
Rare to be found or seen.

Elloc, Lincolnshire

Here lies my wife in earthly mould
Who when she lived did nought but scold.
Peace? wake her not for now she's still;
She had, but now I have my will.

Cherening-le-Clay, Dorset

Who far beneath this tomb doth rest,
Has joined the army of the blest.
The Lord has Ta'en her to the Sky,
The Saints rejoice – and so do I.

Painswick, Gloucestershire

My wife is dead, and here she lies
Nobody laughs, nobody cries;
Where she has gone, or how she fares,
Nobody knows, and nobody cares.

William Joy Home, Carpenter, 1736

*(To the memory of my four wives, who all died within the
space of ten years)*
Dear Wifes if you & I shall go to heaven
The Lord be blest, for then we shall be even.

23

Wolstanton, Staffordshire

Ann Jennings

Some have children – Some had none –
Here lies the mother of twenty-one.

From the London Magazine, 1824

Here lies, thank God, a woman who
Quarrelled & stormed her whole life through;
Tread gently o'er her mouldering form,
Or else you'll cause another storm.

St. Cue, Cornwall

Jane Carthew

Here lies the body of Joan Carthew,
Born at St. Columb, died at St. Cue
Children she had five.
Three are dead & two are alive.
Those that are dead choosing rather
To die with their mother, than live with their father.

St. Mary Key, Ipswich, Suffolk

Joan Trueman

Here lyes crafty Joan, deny it who can
Who liv'd a false maid, & dy'd a Trueman;
And this trick she had to make up her cunning,
Whilst one leg stood still, the other was running.

St. Peter's, Barton, Lincolnshire

Nameless Lady

Doomed to receive half my soul held dear,
The other half with grief she left me here.
Ask not her name, for she was true and just;
Once a fine woman, now a heap of dust.

Shrewsbury, Shropshire

Here lies the body of Martha Dias
Who was always uneasy, and not overpious;
She lived to the age of three score and ten,
And gave to the worms she refused to the men.

Evesham, Worcestershire

Here doth lie
All that can dy
Of Ann Haines who ended this life . . . May 1717

Rhagader, Radnorshire, Wales

I plant these shrubs upon your grave, dear wife,
That something on this spot may boast of life.
Shrubs must wither and all earth must rot;
Shrubs may revive: but you, thank heaven, will not.

Launceston, Cornwall

Sarah Ruddle, 1667

Blest soul since thou art fled into the slumbers of the
dead.
        Why should mine eyes
Let fall unfruitful tears, the offspring of despair and
fears,
        To interrupt the obsequies.
No, No, I won't lament to see thy day of trouble
spents
        But since thou art gone,
Farewell! sleep, take thy rest, upon a better hus-
bands breast
        Until the resurrection.

Somewhere in London

        Constance Bevon, wife of John
        Lies beneath this marble stone;
        Fat and buxom, round and stout,
        'Twas apoplexy bowled her out.

Here is the last long resting-place of dear Jemimer's
  bones;
Her soul ascended into space amidst our tears and
  groans.
She was not pleasing to the eye, nor had she any
  brain,
And when she talked 'twas through her nose, which
  gave her friends much pain.
But still we feel that she was worth the money that
  was spent
Upon the coffin and the hearse (the mourning
  plumes were lent).

Pentewan, Cornwall

In this heare grave you see beforce
Lies buried up a dismos story;
A young maiden she was cross'd in love,
And taken to the realms above.
But he that cross'd her, I should say,
Deserves to go the other way.

Burlington, Shropshire

Here lies the body of Mary Ann Lowder
She burst while drinking a seidlitz powder.
Called from this world to her heavenly rest,
She should have waited till it effervesced.

Gloucester

Beneath this dust lies the smouldering crust
Of Eleanor Batchelor Shoven.
Well versed in the arts of pies, puddings, and tarts
And the lucrative trade of the oven.
When she lived long enough she made her last puff,
A puff by her husband much praised.
And now she does lie and makes a dirt pie
And hopes that her crust will be raised.

Bangor, Wales

Martha Snell

Poor Martha Snell, her's gone away,
Her would if her could, but her couldn't stay,
Her had two bad legs and a baddish cough,
But her legs it was that carried her off.

Mary Anne has gone to rest,
Safe at last on Abraham's breast,
Which may be nuts for Mary Anne,
But is certainly rough on Abraham.

At Church Creton, Salop

On a Thursday she was born,
On a Thursday made a bride,
On a Thursday put to bed,
On a Thursday broke her leg, and
On a Thursday died.

Bedwelty, near Tredegar, Wales

On the Tombstone of a Wife

This poor man wept and the Lord heard him,
and delivered him out of all his troubles.

Gentle Reader, Gentle Reader,
Look on the spot where I do lie,
I was always a very good feeder
But now the worms do feed on I.

Gloucestershire

Here I lie with my three daughters
Who died drinking Cheltenham waters.
If we had stuck to Epsom Salt,
We should not sleep in this cold vault.

Hertfordshire

The Dame, who lies interred within this tomb
Had Rachel's charms and Leah's fruitful womb,
Ruth's filial love, and Lydia's faithful heart,
Martha's just care, and Mary's better part.

Here lies Elizabeth Wise
Who died of thunder sent from Heaven
In 1777.

York Cathedral, Yorkshire

O merciful Jesu, that brought Man Sowl from Hell
Have Merci on the Sowl of Jane Bell.

On a Farmer's Daughter whose Name was Letitia

Grim death, to please his liquorish palate
Has taken my Lettice to put in his sallat.

Ancrum Moor, Roxburgh

Fair Maiden Lilliard lies under this stone
Little was her stature, but great was her fame.
Upon the English lions she had laid many thumps,
And when her legs was cutted off, she fought upon
   her stumps.
            (Battle of Ancrum Moor, 1544)

BERKSHIRE

Reading

William Gordon

Here lies the body of William Gordon;
He had a mouth almighty & teeth accordin';
Stranger, tread lightly on this sod,
For if he gapes, you're gone, by G--.

Easthamstead

Elija Fenton, 1730

This modest stone, which few vain Marbles can,
May truly say, Here lies an honest Man.

Swallowfield

Here lies a fair blossom mould'ring to dust,
Ascending to heaven, to dwell withe the just

Windsor

When this you see remember me
As I lay under ground,
The world say what it will of me,
Speak of me as you have found.

BUCKINGHAMSHIRE

High Wycombe

Death is a fisherman; the world we see
A fish-pond is, and we the fishes be;
He sometimes angles, like doth with us play,
And slyly take us, one by one, away.

Iver

Richard Carter

An honest man, a friend sincere
What more can be said? He's buried here.

Wing Church

Thomas Cotes, 1648

Honest old Tom Cotes that sometimes was
Porter at Ascot Hall, has now alas!
Left his key, lodge, fyre, friends, and all to have
A room in Heaven. This is that good man's grave,
Reader, prepare for thine, for none can tell,
But that you two may meet to-night. Farewell!

Hanslape

On a Prize Fighter

Alexander McKat, 1830

Strong and athletic was my frame
Far from my natives home I came,
And manly fought with Simon Byrne;
Alas! but lived not to return.
Reader, take warning by my fate
Lest you should rue your case too late;
If you have ever fought before,
Determine now to fight no more.

CHESHIRE

Chester

On a Sexton

Hurra! my brave boys
Let's rejoice at his fall!
For if he had lived,
He had buried us all.

Over Peover

Philip and Ellen Mainwaring

Lyke as this marble now does hyde
the bodies of theisse twayne,
So shall not thou on earth lyve longe
but turne to dust agayne.
Then learn to dye and dye to lyve
As theisse two heave example gyve.

Weston

On a Parish Clerk

There lies entombed within this vault so dark,
A Tailor, clothdraw'r, soldier, and a clerk.
Death snatch'd him hence, and also from him took
His needle, thimble, sword, and prayer book.
He could not work nor fight, what then?
He left the world, and faintly cry'd – Amen.

CORNWALL

Acton

Roger Morton

Here lies entombed one Roger Morton
Whose sudden death was early brought on;
Trying one day his corn to mow off,
The razor slipped and cut his toe off.
The toe or rather what it grew too
An information (?inflammation) quickly flew to;
The pants they took to mortifying,
And poor dear Roger took to dying.

Calstock

On a Pedlar

I lodged have in many Town
And travelled many a year,
Till Age & Death have brought me down
To my last lodging here.

James Berlinner, 1844

(He was killed by falling from a haystack)

Consider well both old and young
Who by my grave may pass.
Death soon may come with his keen scythe
And cut you down like grass.
Though some of you perhaps may think
From danger you be free,
Yet in a moment may be sent
Into the grave like me.

Dunheved

George Warrington, 1727

This is my request
My bones may rest
Within this chest
Without molest.

Mousehole

St. Paul's Churchyard

Dolly Pentreath

Old Doll Pentreath, one hundred age and two
Both born, & in Paul Parish buried too;
Not in the Church 'mongst People great and high,
But in the Church-yard doth old Dolly lie!

South Petherwin

Beneath this stone lies Humphrey and Joan,
Who together rest in peace.
Living indeed,
They disagreed,
But now all quarrels cease.

Penryn

Here lies William Smith,
And what is somewhat rarish,
He was born, bred, and
Hanged in this parish.

CUMBERLAND

Rockcliffe

Brough Marsh

Underneath this humble stone
Sleeps a skull of one unknown
Deep in Eden's bed 'twas found,
Was the luckless owner drowned?
What matter, since we all must die,
Whether death be wet or dry.

Wetheral, Carlisle

John Hodgson

He was for 56 years clerk under different clergy

Never missed a Sunday's Service
Present at 5013 christenings
Present at 2112 marriages
Present at 4699 funerals.

Joseph Glendowing, 1808

Murdered near this town June 15, 1808
His murderers were never discovered.
You villains! if this stone you see
Remember that you murdered me!
You bruised my head and pierced my heart
Also my bowels did suffer part.

DEVONSHIRE

West Down

1797

Reader, pass on, nor waste your precious time
On bad biography and murdered rhyme;
What I was before's well known to my neighbours
What I am now is no concern of yours.

Plymouth

Thomas Vernon, 1753

Here lies the body of
Thomas Vernon
The only surviving son
of
Admiral Vernon
Died 23rd July 1753

Widecombe-in-the-Moor

1776

The Rose is red: ye Grass is green:
The Days are past which I have seen.
All ye on me Cast an Eye:
As you are now, so once was I.
But as I am now so shall ye be
Prepare for Death and follow me.

Affington

On Thomas Huddlestone

Here lies Thomas Huddlestone, Reader don't smile!
But reflect, as this tomb-stone you view,
That death, who kill's him, in a very short while
Will huddle a stone upon you.

Stoke, St. Nectan

Stay awhile you passers by
And see how I in dust do lie.
Tho' I lie here in confusing mould
I shall rise up like shining gold.

43

Bideford

Here lies the Landlord of "The Lion"
His hopes removed to lands of Sion
His wife resigned to Heaven's will,
Will carry on the business still.

(Two years later)

Here lies the Landlord's loving wife,
Her soul removed from lands of strife.
She's gone aloft her spouse to tell
The Inn he left her turned out well.

Wiveliscome

On a Brickmaker

James Pady

Keep death and Judgement always in your eye,
Or else the devil off with you will fly,
And in his kiln with brimstone ever fry.
If you neglect the narrow road to seek
Christ will reject you, like a half-burnt brick.

Lillington

I poorly lived, I poorly died
And when I was buried nobody cried.

DURHAM

Beldington

Robert Burrows

Poems & epitaphs are but stuff
Here lies Robert Burrows, that's enough.

Hartlepool

On a Child

A pin stuck in my throat
Which did cause me to choke.

Gateshead

On an Architect

Here lies Robert Trollop
Who made yon stones roll up.
When Death took his soul up,
His body filled this hole up.

45

ESSEX

Chigwell

This disease you ne'er heard tell on, –
I died of eating too much melon;
Be careful, then, all you that feed – I
Suffered because I was too greedy.

Brentwood

Here lies Izaac Greentree

There is a time when these green trees shall fall,
And Izaac Greentree rise above them all.

Great Coggeshall

To the Memory of Thomas Hanse

"Lord the grass is free, – why not for me?"
(A creditor who was ruined by Mr Hanse wrote under it:)

And the Lord answered and said, –
"Because thy debts a'nt paid."

GLOUCESTERSHIRE

Near Bristol

On a Hussar

I went and listed the Tenth Hussars,
And golloped with them to the bloody wars.
"Die for your sovereign – for your country die"
To earn such glory feeling rather shy.
Sung I slipped home, but death soon sent me off
After a struggle with the hooping cough.

Cheltenham

John Adam

Here lies John Adam, who received a thump,
Right on the forehead from the Parish Pump.
Which gave him the quietus in the end,
Though many doctors did this case attend.

Painswick

My time was come! My days were spent!
I was called – and away I went!!!

Buknor

In pain & sickness long I lay,
My flesh & lungs consumed away,
Much like a rose I once did bloom
But now lie mouldering in the tomb.

HAMPSHIRE

Winchester

Thomas Thetcher, 1764

Here sleeps in peace a Hampshire Grenadier
Who caught his death by drinking cold small Beer.
Soldiers be wise from his untimely fall,
And when ye're hot drink strong or none at all.

Winchester

To all my friends I bid adieu;
A more sudden death you never knew;
As I was leading the old mare to drink,
She kicked & killed me quicker'n a wink.

HERTFORDSHIRE

Hertford

Woman

Grieve not for me, my husband dear,
I am not dead, but sleepest here,
With patience wait, prepare to die,
And in a short time you'll come to I.

Husband (Sometime later)

I am not grieved my dearest life;
Sleep on, I have another wife;
Therefore, I cannot come to thee,
For I must go and live with she.

KENT

Sevenoaks

Grim Death took me without any warning,
I was well at night, & dead at nine in the morning.

Eastwell

FEAR GOD

Keep the Commandment
And
Don't attempt to climb a tree,
For that's what caused the death of me.

Canterbury

Touch not my grave, my bones, not yet my dust,
But let this stone which stands, be rotten first.

Chatham

Weep not for me, the warmest tear that's shed
Falls unavailing o'er the unconscious dead;
Take the advice the friendly lines would give,
Live not to drink, but only drink to live.

Tonbridge

Hail!
This stone marks the spot
Where a notorious sot
Doth lie:
Whether at rest or not
It matters not to you or I.

Great Chart

Nicholas Toke

He married five wives whom he survived. At the
age of 93 he walked to London to seek a sixth but
died before he found her.

LANCASHIRE

Rochdale

John and Mary Collier, 1786

Here lies John & with him Mary
Cheek by Jowl they never vary.
No wonder they so well agree,
He wants no punch & Moll no tea.

Liverpool

Poor John lies buried here;
Although he was both hale and stout,
Death stretched him on the bitter bier
In another world he hops about.

Caton

John Berry

Here lies Squire Berry
Who never would marry,
Nor ever gave ought to the poor.
He lived like a Hog,
And died like a Dog,
And left all he had to a W – – – e.

Manchester

My death did come to pass
Thro' sitting on the derty grass;
Here I lie where I fell,
If you seek my soul go to Hell.

Manchester

Here lies John Hill
A man of skill,
His age was five times ten.
He never did good,
Nor ever would,
Had he ever lived as long again.

LEICESTERSHIRE

Barrow-on-Soar

On a Man called Cave

Here in this grave there lies a Cave,
We call a Cave a Grave, –
If Cave be Grave and Grave be Cave,
Then reader judge, I Crave,
Whether doth Cave here lie in Grave,
Or Grave here lie in Cave;
If Grave in Cave here buried lie,
Then Grave where is thy Victory?
Go reader, & report, here lies a Cave
Who conquers Death and buries his own Grave.

LINCOLNSHIRE

Barton

1777

Doomed to receive half my soul held dear,
The other half with grief she left me here.
Ask not her name, for she was true & just;
Once a fine woman, now a heap of dust.

Stamford

William Pepper, 1783

Tho' hot my name, yet mild my nature,
I bore good will to every creature;
I brewed good ale & sold it too,
And unto each I gave his due.

Croyland

Abraham and Mary Baby
and two Children

Man's life is like unto a winter's day
Some break their fast, and so depart away.
Others stay dinner – then depart full fed,
The longest age but sups and goes to bed.
  O reader, then behold and see
  As we are now so must ye be.

Somewhere in Lincolnshire

John Miles

This tombstone is a Milestone:
Ha! How so?
Because beneath lies Miles,
Who's Miles below.

LONDON AREA

Stepney

William Wheatley, 1683

Whoever treadeth on this stone
I pray you tread most neatly;
For underneath the same doth lie
Your honest friend, Will Wheatley.

Camden

John Calf

O cruell Death, as subtle as a fox,
Who would not let this calf live till he's been an Oxe
That he might have eaten both brambles and thorns,
And when he came to his father's years might have
   worn horns.

Hackney

Peter Stiller

And still as death poor Peter lies
And Stiller when alive was he.
Still not without a hope to rise
Thou Stiller then he still will be.

Whitechapel

On an Executioner

Richard Brandon, 17th Century

Who do you think lies buried here?
One that did help to make hemp dear;
The poorest subject did abhor him,
And yet his kind did kneel before him;
He would his master not betray,
Yet he his master did destroy;
And yet no Judas: In records tis found
Judas had thirty pence, he thirty pound.

Hendon

Mr Sand

Who would live by other's breath?
Fame deceives the dead man's trust.
Even our names may change by death,
Sand I was, but now am Dust.

All Hallows, Staining

Colman, 1670

(He was executed in the reign of Charles II)

If Heaven be pleased, when Sinners cease to sin,
If Hell be pleased, when Souls are damn'd therein;
If Earth be pleased, when its rid of a Knave;
Then all are pleased, for Colman's in his Grave.

Micklehurst Churchyard

Life is an Inn, where all men bait,
The waiter Time, the landlord Fate;
Death is the score by all men due,
I've paid my shot – and so must you.

Temple Church

John White

Here lies a John, a burning shining Light,
Whose Name, Life, Actions, were alike, all White.

Somewhere in London

Stop reader! I left the world
In which there was the world to do;
Fretting & stewing to be rich –
Just such a fool as you.

St. Giles, Cripplegate

Gervase Aire

Underneath this marble fair,
Lies the body entomb'd of Gervase Aire:
He dyed not of an agu fit,
Nor surfeited by too much wit.
Methinks this was a wondrous death,
That Air should die for want of breath.

St. Dunstan's Stepney

> Here lies the Body of Daniel Saul
> Spittlefield Weaver, and that's all.

St. Michael's, Crooked Lane

> Here lies wrapt in Clay
> The Body of William Wray
> I have no more to say.

Bishopsgate

John Taylor, 1710

All you that chance this tomb of mine to see,
Pray stop, & read, & warning take by me.
With care observe your parents' sound advice,
Your safety in your just obedience lies.
If you their wise commands once disobey,
Like me, to sudden death you'll fall a prey.

St. Dunstan's in the West

Alexander Layton (Master of Defence) 1679

His Trusts like Lightning flew, but skilful Death
Parry'd 'em all, and put him out of Breath.

Kensington

Thomas Wright, 1776

Farewell, vain world! I've had enough of thee;
I value not what thou canst say of me;
Thy smiles I value not, nor frowns don't fear;
All's one to me, my head is quiet here.
What faults you've seen in me, take care to shun,
Go home, and see there's something to be done.

Rotherhithe

Capt. Thomas Stone, 1666

As the Earth the Earth doth Cover
So under this Stone lies another.

WESTMINSTER ABBEY

Samuel Foote

Here lies one Foote, whose death may thousands
   save,
For death has now one foot within the grave.

John Ellis

Life's uncertain, Death is sure
Sin's the wound, and Christ's the cure

Aphra Behn, 1689

Here lies a Proof that Wit can never be
Defence enough against Mortality.

John Gay, 1732

Life is a jest & all things shew it
I thought so once, but now I know it.

Woodlon

John Racket

Here lies John Racket
In his wooden jacket,
He kept neither horses nor mules;
He lived like a hog
He died like a dog
And left all his money to fools.

Walcott

William Wiseman

Here lies the body of W.W.
He comes no more to trouble U,
Where he's gone or how he fares,
Nobody knows & nobody cares.

Peterborough Cathedral

Here lyes a Babe, that only cry'd
In Baptism to be washt from Sin, and dy'd

Newark

From earth my body first arose,
And now to earth again it goes:
I ne'er desire to have it more,
To tease me as it did before.

NOTTINGHAMSHIRE

Edwalton

Rebecca Freeland, 1741

She drank good ale, good punch and wine
And lived to the age of nine-nine

Selston

On a Gypsy King

I've lodged in many a town
I've travelled many a year,
But death at length has brought me down
To my last lodging here.

Hichling

1727

You readers all both old and young
Your time on earth will not be long
For death will come and die you must
And like to me return to dust.

OXFORDSHIRE

Bensington

On an Infant, two Years of Age

The railing world turn'd poet, made a play,
I came to see it, dislik'd, and went away.

Great Milton

1654

Here lie mother and babe both without sins
Next birth will make her and her infant twins.

STAFFORDSHIRE

Lichfield

Live well – die never
Die well – live forever

SUFFOLK

Lowestoft

In Memory of
Charles Ward
Who died May 1770
aged 63 years
a dutiful son, a loving brother
And an affectionate husband.
N.B. This stone was not erected by Susan his wife.
She erected a stone to John Slater, her second hus-
band, forgetting the affection of Charles Ward, her
first husband.
Let no one disturb his bones.

Since I was so quickly done for,
I wonder what I was begun for.

St. Mary Key, Ipswich

John Warner, 1641

I Warner was to myself
Now Warning am to thee
Both living,,dying, dead I was,
See then thou warned be.

SURREY

Guildford

Reader, pass on, ne'er waste your time
On bad biography and bitter rhyme;
For what I am, this cumb'rous clay insures,
And what I was is no affair of yours.

Somewhere in Surrey

Here rests a fine woman which was sent from above
To teach virtue & graces to men;
But God, when He saw her in very bad hands
Recalled her to heaven again.

Chobham

On an Architect

John Alexander, 1757

Houses he built, with Brick, with Wood and Stone;
But all his art could not support his own;
Death push'd, he strove, vain was ye weak essay;

Down dropt at last his tenement of clay;
Flatt as himself his houses time will throw;
That John e'er lived what mortal then will know;
Yes, or one fabric he consigned to fame;
The lasting fabric of an honest name.

Ockham

On a Woodcutter, 1736

The Lord saw good, I was lopping off wood,
And down fell from the tree;
I met with a check, and I broke my neck
And so death lopp'd off me.

SUSSEX

Chichester

On a Good Soldier

Here lies an old Soldier who all must applaud,
Since he suffer'd much hardship at home & abroad,
But the hardest engagement he ever was in,
Was the Battle of Self in conquest of Sin.

Hastings

Joseph Dain, 1751

Good people as you passed by
I pray you on me cast an eye
For as you are so once was I
And as I am so must you be
Therefore prepare to follow me.

Storrington

Edward Hide

Here lies the body of Edward Hide
We laid him here because he died.

We had rather
It had been his father;
If it had been his sister
We should not have miss'd her.
But since 'tis honest Ned
No more shall be said.

Brighton

His fate was hard, but God's decree
Was drown'd he should lie – in the sea.

Midhurst

Beneath this stone
Lies my wife, Joan,
To h—l she's gone, no doubt
For if she be not,
If heaven's her lot
I must (God wot) turn out.

WARWICKSHIRE

Coleshill

On a Man who had a very wide Mouth

Here lies a man, as God shall me save,
Whose mouth was wide, as is his grave;
Reader tread lightly o'er his sod,
For, if he gapes, you're gone, by G–d.

Coventry

On a Racer

Here lies the swift racer, so famed for his running,
In spite of his boasting, his swiftness & cunning;
In leaping o'er ditches, & slipping o'er fields
Death soon o'ertook him & tript up his heels.

St. Philip's, Birmingham

James Baker, 1781

O cruel Death, how could you be so unkind
To take him before & leave me behind?
You should have taken both of us if either,
Which would have been more pleasant to the
  survivor.

WESTMORLAND

Troutbeck

Here lies a woman,
No man can deny it,
She died in peace, although she lived unquiet;
Her husband prays, if e'er this way you walk,
You would tread softly – if she wake she'll talk.

WILTSHIRE

Near Salisbury

On a Cricketer

I bowl'd, I struck, I caught, I stopp'd
Sure life's a game of cricket;
I block'd with care, with caution popp'd
Yet Death has hit my wicket.

Crudwell

Received of Philip Harding
his borrowed earth
July 4th, 1673

Hindon

Mary Sturgold

Death did to me short warning give,
Therefore be careful how you live;
My weeping friends I left behind,
And had no time to speak my mind!
In the morning I was well,
In the afternoon from cart I fell,
An accident somewhat severe,
In less than a fortnight brought me here.

WORCESTERSHIRE

Worcester

Mammy and I together lived
Just two years & a half;
She went first & I followed after,
The cow before the calf.

On Mr John Mole

Beneath this cold stone lies a son of the earth;
His story is short, though we date from his birth;
His mind was a gross, as his body was big;
He drank like a fish, and he ate like a pig.
No cares of religion, of wedlock, or state,
Did e'er for a moment encumbe John's pate.
He sat or he walked, but his walk was but creeping,
And he rose from his bed – when quite tired of
    sleeping.
Without fee, without friend, unnotic'd he died;
Not a single soul laughed, not a single soul cried.
Like his four-footed namesake, he dearly lov'd earth,
So the sexton has covered his body with turf.

Bromsgrove

Punning Epitaph on a Man called Knott.

Here lies a man that was Knott born
His father was Knott before him.
He lived Knott, and did Knott die,
Yet underneath this stone does lie;
Knott christened,
Knott begot,
And here he lies,
And yet was Knott.

YORKSHIRE

Ripon

Bryan Tunstal, 1790

Here lies poor, but honest Bryan Tunstal; he was a most expert angler, until Death, envious of his Merit, threw out his line, hook'd him, and landed him here the 21st day of April 1790.

Selby

1706

Here lies the body of poor Frank Row,
Parish clerk and grave stone cutter.
And this is writ to let you know,
What Frank for others us'd to do
Is now for Frank done by another.

ISLE OF THANET

George Hill

Against his will
Here lies George Hill
Who from a cliff
Fell down quite stiff.
When it happened is not known,
Therefore not mentioned on this stone.

ISLE OF WIGHT

Ryde

There was an old lady from Ryde
Who ate some apples and died.
The apples fermented inside the lamented,
Made cider inside her inside.

Whippingham

Thomas Burnett, 1842

At midnight he was call'd away
From his employment on the sea, –
Although his warning was but short,
We hope he's reached the heavenly port.

St. Nicholas' Churchyard, Yarmouth

Here lies one, a sailor's bride
Who widowed was because of the tide;
It drowned her husband – so she died.

IRELAND

Belturbet

Here lies John Higley, whose father and mother were drowned on their passage from America. Had both lived, they would have been buried here.

Somewhere in Ireland

On a Grocer

Here lie the remains of John Hall, grocer
The world is not worth a fig, and I have good raisins
   for saying so.

Cork

Patrick Steel

Here lies Patrick Steel;
That's very true!
Who was he! What was he!
What's that to you?
He lies here, because he
Is dead – nothing new.

Dundalk

Here lies the body of Robert Moore,
What signifies more words?
Who killed himself by eating curds.
But if h'd been ruled by Sarah his wife,
He might have lived all the days of his life.

SCOTLAND

Stirling

Janet Reid

Janet Reids body does lie here,
Who died by drinking Aithree water.
If she'd stuck to beer, of the guid strong & clear,
She'd been alive & nothing the matter.

Wigtown, Wigtownshire

Here lies John Taggart of honest fame
Of stature low, and leg lame;
Content he was with portion small,
Kept a shop in Wigton, and thats all.

Necropolis, Glasgow

Here lies Bessy Bell
What whereabouts I cannot tell.

WALES

Caernarvon, Caernarvonshire

On a Doctor and Body Snatcher

Many I've raised from the grave
And pickled for dissection.
Saved in my turn I hope to have
A glorious resurrection.

Montgomery, Montgomeryshire

All you that come our grave to see
A moment pause and think.
How we are in eternity
And you are on the brink.

Llangerrig, Montgomeryshire

From earth my body first arose,
But here to earth again it goes.
I never desire to have it more
To plague me as it did before.

Wrexham, Denbighshire

Richard Kendrick

Was buried August 29th, 1785
By the Desire of his wife
Margaret Kendrick

In a churchyard near Llanymyneck

In crossing o'er the fatal bridge
John Morgan he was slain.
But it was not by mortal hand
But by a railway train.

Chepstow

Rev. Chest, 1690

Here lies at rest I do protest
One Chest within another;
The chest of wood was very good
Who says so of the other.

Here lies a man, who from his birth
Was to the world of little worth;
He drank his substance in potions deep
Earth, o Earth! the drunkard safely keep.

FROM FAR AWAY

Some British Exports

AUSTRALIA

Tasmania

Underneath this pile of stones
Lie the remains of Mary Jones.
Her name was Lloyd, it was not Jones,
But Jones was put to rhyme with stones.

Somewhere in Australia

God took our flower – our little Nell,
He thought He too would like a smell.

Delhi, INDIA

Major Eagle, 1811

Silent grave, to thee I trust
This precious pile of worthy dust,
Keep it safe in the sacred tomb,
Until a wife shall ask for room.

MALTA

Rev. John Tyrwitt, 1828

Here lies John Tyrwitt
A learned divine.
He died in a fit
Through drinking port wine.

UNITED STATES OF AMERICA

Connecticut

Mrs Shute, 1840

Here lies cut down like unripe fruit
The wife of Deacon Amos Shute.
She died of drinking too much coffee
Anno Domini eighteen forty

New Jersey

John Sykes

Weep stranger, for a father spill'd
From a stage coach & thereby kill'd;
His name was John Sykes, a maker of sassengers,
Slain with three other outside passengers.

Somewhere in U.S.A.

Beneath this stone, a lump of clay,
Lies Uncle Peter Dan'els
Who, early in the month of May,
Took off his winter flannels.

Burlington, Iowa

Beneath this stone our baby lays
He neither cries nor hollers
He lived just one and twenty days,
And cost us forty dollars.

Keysville, New York

Sarah Thomas is dead

And that is enough,
The candle is out
Also the snuff.
Her soul is in Heaven,
You need not feer
And all that's left
Is interred here.

Burlington, Massachusetts

Sacred to the memory of Anthony Drake,
Who died for peace and quietness sake;
His wife was constantly scolding and scoffin',
So he thought for repose in a twelve-dollar coffin.

Somewhere in U.S.A.

Little Willy in the best of sashes
Played with fire and was burnt to ashes!
Very soon the room got chilly,
But no one liked to poke poor Willie!

TRUTH AND FICTION

(A mixed bag of verified and unverified epitaphs)

Here lies Rev. A- B-
For many years Missionary in B- district.
He was accidentally shot by his native servant.
"WELL DONE, THOU GOOD AND
FAITHFUL SERVANT"

Dr. J. Letsome

When people's ill, they come to I,
I physics, bleeds, and sweats 'em;
Sometimes they live, sometimes they die;
What's that to I? I Letsome (Lets 'em)

An Epitaph to a Man named Willing

Death will'd that Willing here should lie,
Although unwilling here to die.

On a Bone Collector

William Jones

Here lie the bones of William Jones
Who when alive collected bones,
But Death, that grisly bony spectre,
That most amazing bones collector,
Has boned poor Jones so snug and tidy,
That here he lies in bona fide.

Walter Ralegh

Here lyeth Walter Ralegh that arrant villain
That would sell any friend he had for a shilling.

On a poet

Here lies the Lyric, who, with tale & song
Did life three score & ten prolong,
His tale was pleasant & his song was sweet;
His heart was cheerful – but his thirst was great.
Grieve, Reader! grieve that he too soon grown old,
His song has ended and his tale is told.

On John Death

Here lies John Death the very same
That went away with a cousin of his name.

On an Angler

He angled many a purling brook,
But lacked the angler's skill:
He lied about the fish he took,
And here he's lying still.

Sir John Vanbrugh, 1726

Lie light upon him, earth! tho' he
Laid many a heavy load on thee.

Here lies poor Thomas and his wife
Who had a pretty jarring life;
But all is ended – do you see?
He holds his tong, and so does she.

Written by Robert Burns

On a Henpecked Husband

As father Adam first was fool'd,
A case that's still too common,
Here lies a man a woman ruled
The devil rul'd the woman.

Here lies the body of John Mound
Who was lost at sea and never found.

By a Man on his Wife

Two of my bones have taken a trip, –
My rib is departed, so is my HIP.

Wenninghall Church

Thomas Stevens, 1687

Since nothing is so certain as our death,
And nothing more uncertain than when we breath
Expires, we ought each minute to prepare; Death
sends no summons for, but comes unaware.

On a Lawyer

Mr Strange

Here lies an honest lawyer,
And that is Strange.

A drunkard

The draught is drunk, poor Tip is dead
He's top'd his last and reeled to bed.

On a Juggler

Death came to see thy tricks, and cut in twain
Thy thread. Why did'st not make it whole again?